THE

ABC

OF

JIFFY
COOKERY

WITH DECORATIONS BY
RUTH McCREA

WILDSIDE PRESS

TO THE READER

If you're working by day
And cooking by night,
Or your chores you would keep
Both easy and light,

If you like to eat well
But you cook in a hurry,
If you want to relax
Without bother or worry,

If you yearn to play bridge,
Or the weather's too hot;
Or you simply don't want
To bend over a pot,

You'll find that this book
With occasional rhyme,
Will make cooking pleasant,
And help you save time!

THE EDITOR

Abacadabra,
I'll tell you my charm:
Cook the evening before,
Then cover, and warm!

APPLE SOUP

Preparation time: 20 minutes

4 apples, pared and diced
1/2 cup sugar
Rind of 1 lemon, finely chopped
3 cups hot water
1/2 cup red or white wine
2 tablespoons flour
2 tablespoons cold water
1/2 cup heavy cream

Combine apples, sugar, lemon rind, and hot water. Cook until apples are tender. Add wine. Blend flour and cold water. Thin with a few tablespoons of hot soup. Mix into soup. Simmer 5 minutes. Chill, and add cream before serving. Serves 6.

5

A-1 MEAT LOAF

Preparation time: 1 hour

1 pound lean beef, ground
1 pound pork, ground
1 cup white bread crumbs
Milk
¾ teaspoon mixed herbs
2 eggs
Salt and pepper
¼ cup butter
½ cup cream

Mix beef and pork. Soak bread crumbs in a little milk. Mix the two together. Add herbs. Bind with the 2 eggs, well beaten and well seasoned with salt and pepper. Shape mixture into loaf. Melt butter in a roasting pan and place loaf in it.

Bake in 350° oven for 50 minutes. About 10 minutes before done, add cream to juice around loaf. Serves 4-6.

When making gravy and it seems flat and tasteless, peel an onion, wash well and steep in a cup of boiling water for ten or fifteen minutes. Add the liquid to the gravy, and it will take on a lovely brown color and the flavor of the onion.

ALUMINUM FOIL-BAKED SHAD ROE

Preparation time: 40 minutes

1 pair shad roe
Salt
Black pepper, freshly ground
4 tablespoons butter
3 tablespoons parsley, chopped
2 tablespoons dry white wine
Lemon wedges

Preheat the oven to 350°. Sprinkle the shad roe on all sides with salt and pepper. Cut a rectangle of aluminum foil large enough to enclose the roe envelope-fashion. Spread 3 tablespoons of the butter on the center of the foil and sprinkle with the parsley. Cover the bed of parsley with the roe, dot the roe with the remaining 1 tablespoon of butter. Bring up the edges of the foil.

If desired, 2 tablespoons of wine may be poured over the roe. Seal the foil closely. Bake 20 to 25 minutes, depending on size. Serve with lemon wedges. Serves 2.

Test fish as you do cake with a straw to find out if it is done.

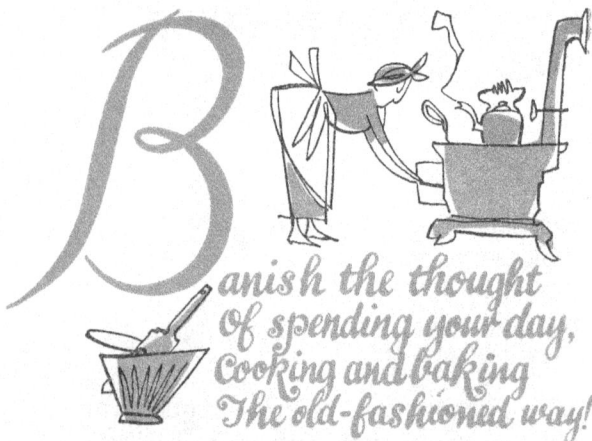

*Banish the thought
Of spending your day,
Cooking and baking
The old-fashioned way!*

BEETS IN SOUR CREAM

Preparation time: 50 minutes

1 pound beets
1/2 cup sour cream
1/2 to 1 tablespoon prepared horseradish
1 teaspoon onion, grated
1/4 teaspoon salt
Chives or parsley, chopped

Cook beets in water to cover until tender. Drain, slip off skins and slice or cube. In the top of a double boiler, mix beets, sour cream, horseradish, onion and salt. Heat, stirring occasionally, to serving temperature. Serve garnished with the chives or parsley. Serves 4.

8

BRAISED CALF'S LIVER

Preparation time: 30 minutes

1½ pounds calf's liver
1 cup onions, finely chopped
¼ cup shortening
1 tablespoon paprika
1 tablespoon tomato paste
½ teaspoon salt

Slice liver in thin, small pieces. Brown the onions in shortening. Stir in the paprika and tomato paste. Add the liver. Cover and simmer over a low flame for 15 minutes, or until the liver is done. Add salt just before serving. Serves 4.

BAKED SOLE

Preparation time: 30 minutes

1 pound fillet of sole
Salt
2 green onions
½ cup white wine
1 tablespoon butter
1 tablespoon flour
1 tablespoon parsley, chopped
½ cup ripe olives, sliced
2 teaspoons lemon juice

Sprinkle fish with salt and arrange in oiled shallow baking dish. Chop onions and

9

sprinkle over fish. Add wine and bake in 400° oven for 15 minutes. Melt butter and add flour.

Drain wine from fish into butter and flour mixture and cook over hot water, stirring until thickened. Add parsley, olives and lemon juice. Pour over fish. Serves 4.

BREADED LAMB STEAKS

Preparation time: 35 minutes

8 half-pound lamb steaks, or
  8 shoulder chops
1 clove garlic
1 teaspoon salt
1/4 teaspoon pepper
Flour
2 eggs, slightly beaten
Bread crumbs
1/2 cup shortening

Trim excess fat from the steaks or chops. Crush garlic and rub over meat; season pieces with salt and pepper and roll in flour. Dip in eggs, then in bread crumbs. Brown quickly on both sides in the hot shortening. Turn heat low and continue cooking slowly, covered, until meat is tender, about 20 minutes. Serves 8.

BAKED SEA BASS
IN WHITE WINE SAUCE

Preparation time: 1 hour

½ cup butter
1 four- to five-pound sea bass
Salt
Black pepper, freshly ground
1 medium onion, chopped
3 tablespoons parsley, finely chopped
1 clove garlic, minced
3 large mushrooms, thinly sliced
2 cups dry white wine
1 tablespoon butter

Preheat the oven to 375°. Butter an oven dish. Dry the fish and season it well inside and out with salt and pepper. Place it in the buttered dish and spread with onion, parsley, garlic and mushrooms. Dot well with the remaining butter except for the 1 tablespoon and pour the wine over all.

Bake 40 to 45 minutes, basting frequently. Remove the fish to a heated platter. Add the 1 tablespoon of cold butter to the sauce in the baking dish. Do not heat. Pour sauce over fish without straining.

Decorate, if desired, with lemon and additional chopped parsley. Serves 6-8.

Chafing-dish cookery
Is the best kind of pal
To a harried young mother
or hard-working gal!

CHILI CON CARNE

Preparation time: 35 minutes

1 onion, diced
1 clove garlic, minced
1 green pepper, diced
2 tablespoons butter
1 pound ground beef
2 cups tomatoes
2 cups canned kidney beans
1 tablespoon chili powder
1 teaspoon sugar
1 teaspoon salt

Sauté onion, garlic and green pepper in butter until tender. Add meat and brown slightly. Add tomatoes, beans, seasonings. Simmer 20 minutes. Serves 4-5.

CURRY SOUP

Preparation time: 20 minutes

2 green apples
2 small onions
4 tablespoons sweet butter
2 cans cream of chicken soup
2 cans milk
1 tablespoon sweet cream
1 teaspoon curry powder

Mince apples and onions finely, and fry in sweet butter until golden brown. Combine chicken soup and milk and bring almost to a boil; add apples and onions, sweet cream and curry powder. Serves 6.

CORNFLAKE OMELET

Preparation time: 20 minutes

2 eggs
1 tablespoon sour cream
Salt and pepper
Dash of chili
2 cups cornflakes, crushed
Several small squares of Cheddar cheese

Beat eggs well with sour cream. Add spices and the crushed cornflakes. Fry on one side and add the cheese squares. Place in broiler and brown. Serves 2.

CARAWAY SEED SOUP

Preparation time: 30 minutes

1 tablespoon caraway seeds
1/2 teaspoon salt
6 cups boiling water
3 tablespoons bacon fat
4 tablespoons flour
1/2 cup sour cream
1/2 cup croutons

Combine the caraway seeds, salt, and water. Simmer for 15 minutes. Blend the fat and flour. Add 2 cups of the soup, and stir until thick and smooth. Combine with the remaining soup and heat to boiling. Divide the cream equally in the soup bowls. Pour the soup over it. Serve with croutons floating on top. Serves 6.

CREAM OF SHRIMP STEW

Preparation time: 1 hour

Combine: 2 cans milk
3 cans cream of shrimp soup (frozen)
2 boxes cleaned, de-veined shrimp (frozen)
4 ounces Sherry

Simmer for 1 hour. Do not boil. Serves 8-10.

CHICKEN LIVERS IN WINE

Preparation time: 20 minutes

1 pound chicken livers
4 tablespoons butter
Flour, salt and pepper
½ cup white wine

Dip livers in flour and fry in butter in skillet or chafing dish. Season with salt and pepper to taste, and add white wine when almost done.

Serve for brunch with scrambled eggs. Serves 4.

CORN AND OYSTERS

Preparation time: 40 minutes

2 cups whole corn
3 eggs, beaten
3 cups white sauce
2 cups oysters
Salt and pepper
Bread crumbs, buttered

Stir corn and eggs into the white sauce. Pour into a casserole and on top arrange well-drained oysters which have been seasoned with salt and pepper. Cover with buttered bread crumbs and bake in a 350° oven for 30 minutes. Serves 6.

Dinner's in the oven,
Getting crisp and brown;
Dad won't be the wiser—
I spent the day in town!

DILL SAUCE

Preparation time: 20 minutes

2 tablespoons butter
2 teaspoons arrowroot
1 cup beef broth
1 tablespoon each: dill weed, wine vinegar
2 tablespoons sugar; 1/2 teaspoon salt
1 egg
1/2 pint sour cream

Melt butter, add arrowroot. Stir until smooth. Add beef broth and boil until creamy; add dill weed, vinegar, sugar, and salt. Remove from heat. Beat egg with sour cream. Add to sauce; heat, serve over bread or potato dumplings. Serves 6.

16

Earth, keep on turning
The minutes to hours;
I've finished the cooking
and I'm fixing the flowers!

EGGS AND SAUSAGE

Preparation time: 15 minutes

8 small sausages
4 eggs, slightly beaten
½ cup cream
Salt and pepper
Green pepper, chopped
Butter for frying

Fry sausages and set aside. Drain off fat. To slightly beaten eggs, add cream, salt and pepper.

Melt butter in pan, add eggs, and scramble lightly. Fold in sausage and chopped green pepper and serve. Serves 4.

EGGS BENEDICT

Preparation time: 30 minutes

4 thin slices ham, fried
4 slices toast, or English muffins
4 eggs, poached
Hollandaise sauce

Arrange slice of fried ham on each piece of buttered muffin or toast. Top with a poached egg and spoon quick Hollandaise sauce over all.

Quick Hollandaise Sauce:

Melt ½ pound butter over hot (not boiling) water. Add 3 egg yolks, ¼ cup lemon juice, ¼ teaspoon salt, 1-2 drops Tabasco sauce (or few grains cayenne pepper) all at once, and beat with rotary beater until thick. Remove from hot water, pour over eggs and serve immediately. Makes generous 1½ cups sauce.

Egg-Boiling Hint:

Always wet egg shells before placing the eggs in water to boil, to prevent cracking. A cracked egg can still be boiled if you rub the cracked spot with moistened salt before placing the egg into boiling water.

EAST INDIAN CURRY SAUCE

Preparation time: 20 minutes

2 tablespoons butter
1 tablespoon onion powder
¾ tablespoon arrowroot
1 tablespoon curry powder
1 teaspoon seasoned salt
¼ teaspoon salt
Dash black pepper
1½ cups milk
1 egg, well beaten

Melt butter over low flame in top of double boiler. Add onion powder and sauté 1 minute. Remove from flame. Mix arrowroot, curry powder, seasoned salt, salt, pepper; blend with butter and onion powder. Combine milk and egg, add to blend. Place over boiling water, stirring constantly until thickened. Serves 6.

Note: To this sauce add 2 cups of any of the following: cubed cold roast lamb, shrimp, chicken, crab, hard-boiled eggs. Serve with steamed white rice, and the usual relishes such as chutney, grated cocoanut, almonds or peanuts, chopped hard-boiled eggs, crisp bacon, finely chopped raw onions.

Fifi, dear Fifi,
What could be more fun,
Than to joke with your guests
With your chores safely done?

FRANKFURTER OMELET

Preparation time: 15 minutes

1 frankfurter, sliced
2 eggs
1 tablespoon sour cream
Salt and pepper

Fry cut slices of frankfurter in butter in frying pan. Beat the eggs well with the sour cream, salt and pepper. Pour over the frankfurters and let fry slowly. When well set place under broiler for 1 minute until brown on top. Serve hot. Serves 1.

Double recipe if there are 2 for lunch. Frankfurter omelet makes a tasty main course for luncheon.

20

Great-Grandmother spent
Her days cooking feasts,
Feeding the chickens
And watering the beasts!

GOURMET LAMB CHOPS

Preparation time: 30 minutes

¾ cup cheese, grated
½ cup fine bread crumbs
½ teaspoon salt
6 thin shoulder lamb chops
1 whole egg, or
  2 egg yolks, beaten

Mix together the cheese, bread crumbs, and salt. Using a pastry brush or spoon, coat the chops on both sides with egg, and dip in the cheese mixture. Arrange on a baking sheet and broil slowly, turning once. When cheese is melted and crumbs brown, meat should be tender. Serves 6.

GERMAN PANCAKE

Preparation time: 30 minutes

4 eggs
½ cup sugar
Pinch of salt
3 tablespoons butter
1 cup flour
½ cup milk

Separate eggs. Beat the egg yolks, sugar, salt, and butter together. Beat in flour and milk a little at a time, till used up. Whip the egg whites and fold in. Pour the mixture into a pan with very hot butter and fry for a few minutes over medium heat.

When lightly browned, turn over, and using 2 forks tear pancake into fairly large-sized pieces, rather roughly. Turn the pieces over and over, shaking the pan, till a nice golden brown is obtained.

Serve hot with sugar sprinkled over. A little cinnamon can be sprinkled also if desired. Serves 4.

German pancakes make a filling dessert for luncheon or a light dinner. Perfect for late suppers or after-the-theater!

GOURMET BAKED OMELET

Preparation time: 30 minutes

6 eggs, separated
2½ teaspoons flour
2½ teaspoons cornstarch
1 cup milk
½ teaspoon salt
⅛ teaspoon pepper
2 tablespoons butter

Mix egg yolks thoroughly with flour and cornstarch. Add milk, salt and pepper gradually. Fold in egg whites, which have been beaten stiff. Melt butter in 9-inch skillet. When hot, pour in egg mixture.

Bake for 20 minutes in 350° oven. Remove from pan and fold on hot platter. Serve with creamed mushrooms, shrimp or chicken; or with jam.

GOURMET BROILED SPARERIBS

Preparation time: 30 minutes

4 pounds spareribs	¼ cup chili powder
3 garlic buds	Worcestershire sauce
1 tablespoon salt	½ cup vinegar

Mix all ingredients and sprinkle on the ribs, then broil or barbecue them. Serves 8.

*Hurry to market
To buy a fat fish;
Then bake him in wine
For an elegant dish!*

HOT LOBSTER CANAPÉS

Preparation time: 20 minutes

1 can lobster
¼ teaspoon paprika
1 teaspoon prepared mustard
½ teaspoon Worcestershire sauce
3 drops Tabasco
3 tablespoons Sherry
½ cup mayonnaise
Toast rounds or crackers

Drain lobster. Mince meat very fine or grind. Add seasonings, Sherry and mayonnaise. Pile mixture on small rounds of toast or crackers and place under broiler until sauce bubbles. Yields 18-25 servings.

24

HERRING SALAD

Preparation time: 20 minutes

3 filleted salt herrings
2 slices cold pork
1 pickled cucumber
2 gherkins
3 apples, peeled and cored
1 cup beetroot, diced
2 cups cooked potato, diced
3/4 cup olive oil
2 tablespoons vinegar
1 teaspoon mustard
1/2 glass white wine
1 onion, chopped
1/2 teaspoon sugar
1/2 teaspoon salt
Pinch white pepper

Chop the salted herrings and pork slices into fairly large pieces. Slice the cucumber and gherkins. Dice the peeled and cored apples. Put all these with the diced beetroot and potatoes into a deep salad bowl.

Mix olive oil, vinegar, mustard, wine, finely chopped onion, sugar, salt and pepper. Pour this mixture over the ingredients in the salad bowl, mix gently and serve cold. Serves 4.

HAM WITH MUSTARD CREAM SAUCE

Preparation time: 35 minutes

2 slices boiled ham, 1/2-3/4-in. thick
4 tablespoons prepared mustard
4 tablespoons brown sugar
1 cup evaporated milk

Place 1 slice of ham in greased baking dish. Mix mustard and brown sugar. Spread half of it on the ham. Top with other slice and spread with rest of prepared mixture.

Cover with evaporated milk and bake in 350° oven for 20-25 minutes, basting frequently. Brown slightly under broiler.

Serve on platter with remaining sauce poured over it. Serves 4.

HAMBURGERS À LA SHERRY

Preparation time: 10 minutes

2 pounds round steak, ground
1/8 pound butter
Salt
Pepper
Bahamian mustard
Sherry

Form patties of the hamburger, using 1/3

26

pound meat to each patty. Heat butter in a frying pan until it is golden brown. Fry the hamburgers until well-browned on a very hot fire, applying salt, pepper and a liberal coating of Bahamian mustard to the exposed raw side of the hamburgers.

Turn over, and pour a little Sherry over each hamburger. Sherry will trickle down and mix with the browned butter to make a delicious gravy. Cook about 5 minutes and serve immediately. Serves 6.

HINTS FOR SOUR CREAM SAUCE

Season sour cream with salt, dry mustard, paprika and lemon juice; use in place of mayonnaise for chicken salad. Or flavor sour cream with orange rind and juice, lemon juice and honey and serve with cut-up fresh fruit. Or turn it into a hot sauce for broccoli, new potatoes, asparagus. Into a tablespoon of melted butter, mixed with a tablespoon of flour, stir 1 cup sour cream. Heat slowly, stir till thickened, then cover and cook over hot water about 5 minutes. Add chopped parsley, if desired.

love a rare steak
Or a succulent chop;
A cinch to prepare:
You can cook on the hop!

ICE CREAM TOPPINGS

Here are a few easy suggestions:

Shaved maple sugar with pecans,
    chopped fine
Chocolate chips
Crushed hard peppermint candy
Crushed macaroons
Slivered semi-sweet chocolate
Various liqueurs (crème de menthe, crème
    de cacao, apricot cordial, etc.), rum,
    brandy
Warm mincemeat (bottled type)
Warmed honey
Hot demi-tasse coffee
Frosted animal crackers (for children).

Jolly the board
With a hostess serene;
a casserole dinner
With just one pot to clean!

JAMBALAYA

Preparation time: 30 minutes

2 tablespoons butter
½ cup celery, chopped
½ cup onion, minced
½ cup green pepper, chopped
2 tablespoons flour
4 tablespoons tomato paste
1¾ cups water
1 teaspoon salt
Pepper
1 pound shrimp, canned or fresh cooked
2 cups cooked rice

Melt butter in a skillet, add celery, onion and green pepper and cook until tender.

Stir in the flour and gradually pour in the tomato paste and water mixed together. Add seasoning and cook 5 minutes longer, stirring constantly. Add shrimp and heat thoroughly. Serve over rice. Serves 6.

JENNY'S LOBSTER STEW

Preparation time: 20 minutes

1 can lobster
4 tablespoons butter
1 teaspoon onion, minced
½ cup celery, diced
2 tablespoons green pepper, minced
½ cup water
1 quart milk, scalded
Salt
Paprika
2 tablespoons parsley, minced

Drain lobster. Reserve liquor, and flake meat. Melt butter. Add onion, celery and green pepper, and cook 2 minutes over low heat. Add water, cover and cook minutes. Add lobster liquor and flake lobster. Heat thoroughly and add scalded milk.

Season to taste with salt and paprika. Add minced parsley. Serve with hot crackers. Serves 4.

JERSEY OMELET

Preparation time: 40 minutes

4 slices bacon
2 tablespoons minced white onions
  soaked in 2 tablespoons water 5 minutes
1 teaspoon shredded parsley
½ teaspoon seasoned salt
4 eggs
½ cup light cream
1 teaspoon seasoned salt
1 teaspoon salt
⅛ teaspoon black pepper
1 cup Swiss cheese, grated
Paprika

Cut bacon slices in two. Fry until partially cooked, but not crisp. Remove from pan. Sauté onion and parsley in drippings until light brown. Season with ½ teaspoon seasoned salt. Spread in 8-inch pie pan. Beat eggs slightly with cream. Season with 1 teaspoon seasoned salt, salt and pepper.

Pour over onions, sprinkle with cheese. Arrange bacon slices on top; sprinkle with paprika. Bake in a 350° oven 15 minutes or until eggs are set and cheese melted. Serves 4.

Kitchens are cozy
and comfy and warm,
But no place to linger
When company's come!

KRAUT

Preparation time: 20 minutes

4 cups cabbage, shredded
4 slices bacon, diced
2 tablespoons brown sugar
1 tablespoon flour
½ cup water
⅓ cup vinegar
salt, pepper
2 cloves
1 small onion, sliced

Cook cabbage in boiling, salted water 7 minutes. Fry bacon. Add sugar and flour to bacon fat; blend. Add water, vinegar, and seasonings; cook until thick. Add onion, bacon, cabbage, and heat. Serves 6.

et's to the baker
To buy us a cake;
I'll mix a fine salad
And broil a quick steak!

LOBSTER SALAD

Preparation time: 10 minutes

1 can lobster, chilled
1½ cups celery, diced
¾ cup mayonnaise
¼ cup sour cream
Salt, paprika
Salad greens
12 ripe olives

Drain chilled lobster, and dice. Add the celery, mayonnaise and sour cream and toss lightly. Add salt and paprika to taste.

Line small salad bowl with crisp salad greens. Pile salad in center and garnish with sliced ripe olives. Yields 4 servings.

LOBSTER NEWBURG

Preparation time: 30 minutes

2 cans lobster
4 tablespoons butter
3 tablespoons flour
½ teaspoon salt
¼ teaspoon nutmeg
1 cup thin cream and lobster liquor
¼ cup Sherry
2 drops Tabasco
3 egg yolks, slightly beaten
Toast points

Drain lobster. Reserve liquor, and dice meat. Melt butter and stir in flour, salt and nutmeg. Add lobster liquor and cream, while stirring constantly over low heat. When sauce thickens, stir in Sherry and Tabasco.

Add diced lobster and cook over low heat until thoroughly heated. Add a little of the hot sauce to beaten egg yolks and mix gently into the lobster mixture. Add more salt, if necessary. Serve garnished with toast points or over slices of toast. Yields 6 servings.

Lobster Newburg is an elegant supper dish, served with dry white rice and a crisp green salad. Just coffee, no dessert!

LOBSTER A LA KING

Preparation time: 20 minutes

1 can lobster
4 tablespoons butter
1 cup fresh, or
  ½ cup canned mushrooms, sliced
2 tablespoons green pepper, sliced
3 tablespoons flour
1 teaspoon salt
⅛ teaspoon pepper
1 cup lobster liquor and milk
½ cup cream
1 tablespoon lemon juice
Halved, toasted English muffins, or
  toast rounds

Drain lobster. Reserve liquor, and flake the meat. Melt butter and add mushrooms and green pepper. Stir constantly over low heat 2 minutes. Stir in the flour and seasonings. Add lobster liquor and milk and cream gradually, while stirring constantly.

Beat in lemon juice and add flaked lobster. Heat thoroughly, and add more salt, if necessary.

Serve over toasted English muffins or toast rounds. Yields 6 medium servings, or 4 generous servings.

35

*Mirth and good cheer
And a small friendly dinner:
You've offered life's best,
And your party's a winner!*

MUSHROOMS AND OYSTERS

Preparation time: 40 minutes

1 cup mushrooms	2 pints oysters
8 Tbs. melted butter	1 cup milk
1 cup fine crumbs	½ cup light cream

Slice mushrooms and sauté in 2 tablespoons butter 2 minutes. Line bottom of greased casserole with ⅓ of crumbs, add a layer of sliced mushrooms and dot with 1 tablespoon butter; add another layer of crumbs, then oysters, remaining sliced mushrooms and a final layer of crumbs.

Pour milk, cream and remaining 5 tablespoons melted butter over top. Bake in 350° oven 25 minutes. Serves 6.

No more weary cooking,
Temper growing hot —
The only one a-stewing
Is the chicken in the pot!

NEW ORLEANS CRABMEAT AND MUSHROOMS

Preparation time: 45 minutes

1 pound crabmeat, fresh or canned
4-ounce can mushrooms
2 tablespoons butter
2 tablespoons flour
½ cup milk
½ cup white wine
1 small onion, grated
½ teaspoon salt
¼ teaspoon curry powder
Bread crumbs

Flake crabmeat. Remove stiff membranes.
Melt butter, remove from heat. Blend in

37

flour. Gradually add milk and wine. Stir until smooth. Add seasonings. Cook over low heat, stirring constantly, about 2 minutes. Add crabmeat and mushrooms.

Place in greased individual casseroles or shells. Sprinkle tops with bread crumbs. Dot with butter. Bake in a 350° oven for 30 minutes. Serves 4.

NOODLE AND HASH CASSEROLE

Preparation time: 50 minutes

1 can peas
Milk
1 tablespoon butter
2 tablespoons flour
Salt
1/2 cup cheese, grated
1/4 teaspoon Tabasco sauce
2 cups noodles, cooked
1 (1-lb.) can corned beef hash

Drain peas; measure liquid and add milk to make 1 1/2 cups. Melt butter, blend in flour and salt. Add liquid mixture and bring to a boil, stirring constantly. Remove from the heat; stir in grated cheese and Tabasco.

Place ¾ cup cooked noodles in the bottom of pan 6 x 10 inches; add a layer of peas, hash and cream sauce. Repeat layers until all ingredients are used, ending with hash in a border around edge. Bake in a 350° oven 30 minutes. Serves 4-6.

NEW ENGLAND
CORN FRITTERS

Preparation time: 20 minutes

1 cup flour, sifted
1½ teaspoons baking powder
½ teaspoon salt
1 egg, well beaten
½ cup milk
1 cup corn, cream style
1 teaspoon onion, grated

Mix and sift flour, baking powder and salt. Combine egg, milk and corn. Stir into flour, mixing until flour is dampened. Add onion. Cover bottom of a hot skillet with a thin layer of shortening. Drop mixture by small spoonsful onto hot pan. Brown on one side, turn over and brown on other.

Cook about 3-4 minutes for small fritters. Serves 6.

ffice slaveys hearken!
Cooking can be fun;
Use your business methods
To get it quickly done!

OYSTERS TERRAPIN

Preparation time: 30 minutes

3 onions, fried in butter
1 pound mushrooms
1 pint oysters
1 recipe white sauce
Sherry to taste
Toast

Add mushrooms to the onions which have been fried until light brown, and cook for about 15 minutes. Combine with 1 pint of raw oysters, and 1 standard recipe of white sauce. Add Sherry. Cook gently a few minutes and serve on toast. Serves 4.

Pretty Bride, listen,
a secret I'll tell;
You can learn to cook quickly,
and learn to cook well!

POTATO PANCAKES

Preparation time: 30 minutes

2 pounds raw potatoes, peeled
1 tablespoon salt
2 tablespoons flour
3 eggs, separated
1 cup milk or cream
Fat for frying

Grate new potatoes into a bowl with cold water. Squeeze through a clean cloth. Add salt, flour, egg yolks and milk, and mix in stiffly beaten egg whites. Drop by tablespoonsful into a frying pan with hot fat. Fry pancakes until golden and crisp. Serves 4-6.

PEA AND TOMATO SOUP

Preparation time: 10 minutes

1 can condensed tomato soup
1 can pea soup
2 cans milk
Cinnamon
Nutmeg
Sherry to taste

Combine tomato and pea soup; add milk, then cinnamon and nutmeg to taste; heat. Just before serving, add Sherry. Serves 6.

POTATO & SPINACH SOUP

Preparation time: 45 minutes

2 medium potatoes, peeled
1 large onion
1 package frozen spinach
1 quart milk
1 teaspoon seasoned salt
1/8 teaspoon garlic powder
Salt and pepper to taste
Pinch nutmeg and mace
2 tablespoons Sherry

Cut up potatoes and onion, cover with water and cook slowly until tender. Also cook spinach 1 minute. Drain all and put through food mill or Waring mixer. If you use mixer, combine vegetables and put in blender in 2 parts. Add ½ cup milk to each part. Then add balance of milk and seasoning, stirring constantly as it reheats. Add Sherry just before serving. Serves 6.

POULET SAUTÉ SEC

Preparation time: 1 hour

1 frying chicken, cut up
Salt, pepper and flour
4 tablespoons butter
2 green onions, chopped
2 tablespoons parsley, chopped
Sprinkle of thyme and basil
½ cup white wine
4 ounces mushrooms, sliced

Dust pieces of chicken with flour seasoned with salt and pepper. Melt butter in a large, heavy skillet; add chicken and sauté until golden brown, turning the pieces frequently and adding more butter, if necessary.

Add onion, parsley, thyme, basil and wine, cover tightly and simmer gently for 30 minutes. Add drained mushrooms; continue cooking for 15 minutes or until chicken is tender and no liquid remains in the pan. Serves 4.

*Quick as a wink,
Quick as a flash —
I'll make you a dinner
With zing and with dash!*

QUICK-AND-EASY PIZZA

Preparation time: 10 minutes

English muffins
Chili sauce
Sharp Cheddar cheese
Spaghetti sauce seasoning

Tear (do not cut) muffins in two, keeping the rounds fairly even. Toast but do not brown the flat sides by placing them at least 5 inches below the broiler flame. Remove from broiler and spread with 1 teaspoon chili sauce. Crisscross thin strips of cheese, over which 1/4 teaspoon spaghetti sauce seasoning is sprinkled. Return to broiler and toast until cheese is melted.

44

ubies and emeralds
Win some women's love;
I'm easy to please —
Just a spanking new stove!

RAISIN PILAU

Preparation time: 20 minutes

1½ teaspoons instant coffee
1½ cups water
1 five-ounce package rice, precooked
½ cup raisins
½ cup walnuts, chopped
⅛ teaspoon salt
⅛ teaspoon nutmeg
½ cup brown sugar, packed
1 cup heavy cream

Mix together instant coffee and water. Using the coffee instead of water, prepare precooked rice according to package directions. Stir in remaining ingredients ex-

45

cept cream. Mix well, and cool. Whip cream and fold into mixture, reserving some for garnish.

Spoon into serving dishes and top with whipped cream and chopped nut meats. Serves 6. May be made the day before. It is excellent for buffets.

RICE AND SHRIMP

Preparation time: 40 minutes

½ pound sharp Cheddar cheese
½ cup evaporated milk
Salt and pepper
3 cups rice, cooked
2 pounds shrimp, cooked
1 cup bread crumbs, buttered

Cut cheese in small pieces; melt over hot water. Gradually stir in milk, beating until smooth; then add seasonings. Pour half of cheese sauce into greased casserole; place half of rice over sauce, cover with shrimp and top with remaining rice.

Pour remaining cheese sauce over all and top with crumbs; bake in 350° oven 15-20 minutes. Serves 8.

ROYAL CRABMEAT

Preparation time: 40 minutes

6 cups potatoes, mashed
3 cups crabmeat, flaked
1½ cups medium white sauce
¾ cup crumbs, buttered
Parsley

Line casserole with mashed potatoes; bake in 400° oven 10 minutes, or until slightly browned. Fill with combined crabmeat and white sauce. Sprinkle with crumbs and return dish to oven for 15 minutes. Garnish with parsley. Serves 8.

ROUMANIAN MUSHROOMS AND SOUR CREAM

Preparation time: 30 minutes

1 pound mushrooms
3 tablespoons butter
1 cup sour cream
Salt and pepper to taste

Wash mushrooms. Place butter in skillet and sauté mushrooms. When tender add sour cream. Cook slowly until sauce is thickened. Season and serve on toast. Serves 4.

Sing while you gather
Your good friends together,
With food and with wine,
Who cares for the weather?

SALMON WITH SAUCE

Preparation time: 30 minutes

Poach salmon in water seasoned with:

½ teaspoon seasoned salt
½ teaspoon parsley, shredded
¼ teaspoon celery seed
1 teaspoon salt
Whole black pepper

and serve either hot or cold with the following sauce:

1 cup sour cream
1 teaspoon dill weed
1 tablespoon wine vinegar
¼ teaspoon sugar
1 teaspoon salt

48

SWEDISH MEAT BALLS

Preparation time: 40 minutes

2/3 cup bread crumbs
1 1/2 cups milk
1 medium onion
4 tablespoons butter
3/4 pound beef, ground
3/4 pound pork, ground
1 egg
2 teaspoons salt
1/4 teaspoon pepper
1/2 cup Sherry

Soak bread crumbs in milk. Then chop onion fine and cook in 1 tablespoon butter until slightly brown. Add meat, onion, unbeaten egg and seasonings to bread crumb mixture. Mix thoroughly.

Now melt another tablespoon butter in a skillet. Form small meat balls by scooping up some of the meat on a teaspoon which has been dipped into the hot fat. Brown meat evenly. Keep shaking the skillet to make meat balls turn over and over. When well browned and thoroughly cooked, transfer to a plate, add remaining butter to skillet and fry remaining meat balls.

Now add about 1/2 cup water to skillet,

add Sherry and all the meat balls. Cook gently over a low heat for about 15 minutes or until all the liquid is absorbed. Makes 6 to 8 servings.

SHERRIED EGGS WITH CHEESE

Preparation time: 20 minutes

1 cup butter
½ cup cream
½ pound Swiss cheese, grated
6 eggs
½ teaspoon salt
3 tablespoons Sherry

Melt ½ cup butter in double boiler. Add cream and heat. Add grated cheese and stir until almost melted. Add slightly mixed eggs and salt.

As eggs are beginning to set, stir from bottom until eggs are lightly scrambled. Then add the rest of the butter and the Sherry.

Serve on toast that has been spread with deviled ham or accompany with grilled ham. Serves 4.

SWISS CHEESE FONDUE

Preparation time: 45 minutes

2 cups milk, scalded
2 cups bread cubes, tightly packed
6 ounces American cheese, diced
1½ tablespoons butter
½ teaspoon salt
¼ teaspoon mustard
3 egg yolks
3 egg whites

Mix the scalded milk with bread cubes, diced cheese, butter, salt and mustard. Beat egg yolks until lemon-colored and blend cheese mixture into egg yolks. Beat egg whites until stiff and fold into first mixture.

Pour into greased baking dish, 10 inches in diameter, and bake in a 350° oven 30 minutes, or until set. Serve immediately. Serves 6.

SOUR CREAM SAUCE

1 pint sour cream
1 teaspoon vanilla
1 tablespoon sugar

Combine ingredients and use in place of whipped cream.

SHRIMP PILAU

Preparation time: 45 minutes

4 slices bacon
2 cups water
1 cup rice
Salt
3 tablespoons butter
½ cup celery, chopped
2 tablespoons green pepper, chopped
1 teaspoon Worcestershire sauce
2 cups shrimp, shelled and de-veined
1 tablespoon flour
Pepper

Cook the bacon until crisp. Dice, add to the water and bring to a boil. Add the rice and ½ teaspoon salt. Cover and cook slowly until the rice is tender, about 15 minutes. Keep hot.

In a separate saucepan, heat the butter, add the celery and green pepper, and cook 3 or 4 minutes. Sprinkle the Worcestershire sauce over the shrimp. Dredge in flour. Add to the celery and green pepper and cook, stirring, 4 or 5 minutes.

Season with salt and pepper. Add the rice and bacon mixture and toss together. Serves 4.

The clock is my enemy,
Its ticking I hate;
I hurry and scurry,
And still dinner's late!

TOMATO ORANGE SOUP

Preparation time: 15 minutes

½ cup onion, finely chopped
2 tablespoons melted butter
6 cups tomato juice
1 teaspoon salt
1 cup orange juice
1 lemon, thinly sliced

Cook onion in butter until tender. Add tomato juice and salt; bring to a boil. Add orange juice and heat to serving temperature. Serve, garnish with slice of lemon. Serves 8.

TOMATO SOUP WITH WINE

Preparation time: 10 minutes

3 cups tomato juice
2 cups white wine
3 tablespoons sugar
2 hard-boiled eggs, sliced

Combine the tomato juice, wine, and sugar. Heat to blend. Chill. Serve with floating slices of egg. Serves 6.

TOMATO-CHEESE PIZZA

Preparation time: 20 minutes

4 English muffins
2 ripe tomatoes, or
   ¾ cup stewed tomatoes, drained
16 anchovy fillets
½ teaspoon rosemary
8 thin slices mozzarella
Olive oil
Salt and pepper

Break apart muffins. Toast until crisp. Thinly slice tomatoes and place 1 slice or 2 tablespoons stewed tomatoes on each muffin half. Then add 2 anchovy fillets and a pinch of rosemary. Add another layer of tomato and top with a slice of

54

mozzarella. Sprinkle with olive oil, salt and pepper.

Place under broiler and broil until mozzarella melts. Serves 4.

TANIA'S ONION SOUP

Preparation time: 40 minutes

2½ cups onions, thinly sliced
2 tablespoons melted butter
2 cans condensed bouillon
2 cans water
2 beef bouillon cubes
¼ teaspoon pepper
6 rounds French bread
¼ cup Parmesan cheese, grated

Sauté onion rings in butter over low heat until yellow. Slowly add bouillon and water. Heat until simmering, then add bouillon cubes and pepper. Cover and cook for 20 minutes. Sprinkle rounds of bread with grated cheese and place under medium broiler heat until golden brown.

Top each serving with a toast round. Serve with grated Parmesan on the side, if desired. Serves 6.

*Unless you have plenty
of time and of leisure,
Prepare in advance
For an evening of pleasure!*

UMBERTO'S CALF'S LIVER

Preparation time: 25 minutes

2 pounds liver, cut into small pieces
3 tablespoons butter
1 onion, chopped fine
2 cloves garlic, minced
Juice of ½ lemon, salt, pepper
¼ cup white wine
1 small can mushrooms
1 tablespoon parsley, chopped

Melt butter, add the onion, garlic, lemon juice, salt, pepper, and liver. Cook for 5 minutes over hot fire, shuffling pan constantly. Add wine, mushrooms and parsley. Cook 3 minutes more. Serves 4.

Verily, verily,
My Man John,
I'm home from the office
And supper is on!

VARIOUS QUICK SANDWICH SPREADS

Anchovy and cream cheese
Caviar and chopped onion and egg
Smoked salmon
Canned salmon, celery, mayonnaise
Crabmeat and mayonnaise
Tuna fish and mayonnaise
Lobster and mayonnaise
Shad roe, mashed with hard-boiled eggs
Ham and Swiss cheese
Tongue and Swiss cheese
Sliced chicken
Chopped chicken liver
Chicken, dill pickle, mayonnaise
Raw beef (Cannibal)

Lamb and lettuce
Salami
Bacon and watercress, cheese or tomato
American cheese and olive
Hot melted cheese
Cream cheese and onion
Beet and egg
Chopped pimiento and olive
Mashed cheese with Worcestershire
Chopped celery and egg
Green pepper, hard-boiled egg, mayonnaise
Banana and chopped walnut
Apple and chopped walnut
Pecans, olives, celery, mixed with mayonnaise
Chopped olive and nuts, salad dressing

VEAL STEAK

Preparation time: 40 minutes

1¼ pound veal steak, sliced ½-inch thick
½ teaspoon salt
¼ teaspoon pepper
3 tablespoons butter

Trim steak, and season. Heat frying pan and melt butter. Place the meat in the melted butter and brown slowly for 25 to 30 minutes, turning from side to side until meat is tender and golden brown. Serve with oven-browned potatoes and a tossed salad. Serves 2-3.

VEAL SCALLOPINE

Preparation time: 25 minutes

1 pound veal cutlet, sliced thin
Flour
6 tablespoons butter
Salt and pepper
¼ cup Sherry
2 tablespoons parsley, chopped
½ can mushrooms, sliced

Dip veal cutlet in flour. Sauté in butter in large skillet, for 3 to 4 minutes on each side. Sprinkle with salt and pepper and add Sherry. Add parsley and mushrooms. Cover and simmer 10 minutes. Serves 4.

VIENNESE RICE

Preparation time: 40 minutes

½ cup uncooked rice
1 (4-oz.) can sliced mushrooms, drained
2 tablespoons butter
1 can onion soup, condensed
½ soup-can water

Brown lightly uncooked rice and sliced mushrooms, which have been drained, in melted butter. Stir in onion soup and water. Cover; cook over low heat about 25 minutes or until rice is tender. Serves 4.

What's the hurry, Madam?
You needn't cook all day;
Forget old-fashioned methods
and cook the "jiffy" way!

WINE FLAVORED FISH FILLETS

Preparation time: 30 minutes

1 each: carrot, celery stalk, onion
2 sprigs parsley, chopped
2 tablespoons butter
2 pounds fish fillets
1 cup white wine
Salt, pepper

Slice the vegetables, and simmer in butter until nearly done. Cut fish fillets in serving pieces and arrange over vegetables. Pour on the wine, and season. Cook covered over low heat until fish is tender and sauce is slightly thickened. Serves 6.

60

ounds, said the Duchess
My friends have brought friends!
And on that cheery note
our little book ends!

X-TRA GOOD CHERRY SOUP

Preparation time: 20 minutes

2 pounds sour cherries, pitted
1 cup or more sugar
1 stick cinnamon
3 cups water
2 tablespoons flour
1 cup heavy cream
1 cup red wine

Simmer cherries, sugar, and cinnamon in water until cherries are tender. Remove cinnamon. Blend flour with 3 tablespoons of cold water. Thin with 3 more tablespoons water and stir into hot soup. Boil. Chill. Stir in cream and wine. Serves 6.